. . . IF YOU LIVED WITH
THE IROQUOIS

BY ELLEN LEVINE
ILLUSTRATED BY SHELLY HEHENBERGER

SCHOLASTIC INC.
NEW YORK   LONDON   TORONTO   AUCKLAND   SYDNEY
MEXICO CITY   NEW DELHI   HONG KONG

ACKNOWLEDGMENTS

With much gratitude to John Kahiones Fadden, a Mohawk of the Turtle Clan, for his careful review of the manuscript, and his generosity and friendship. Many thanks to Gary Van Cour, who introduced me to John Fadden; and to Joe Crank, Mark Cooney, and Harry Orlyk, all of whom shared with me their enthusiasm and their books. The selection from the Thanksgiving Address is reprinted from *Thanksgiving Address: Greetings to the Natural World,* published by the Native Self-Sufficiency Center, the Six Nations Indian Museum, the Tracking Project, and the Tree of Peace Society, PO Box 266, Corrales, New Mexico 87048.

ISBN 0-590-67445-5

Book design by Laurie Williams

12 11 10 9 8 7 6 5 4 3 2 1   8 9/9 0 1 2 3/0

Printed in the U.S.A.

First Scholastic printing, October 1998

CONTENTS

Introduction

Before there was a United States, there were hundreds of thousands, some say millions, of people living on the land between the Atlantic and Pacific Oceans. The most powerful in the Northeast, perhaps in the whole country, were the Haudenosaunee [HO-den-o-SAW-nee], the People of the Longhouse. We know them as the Iroquois.

The Great Iroquois League stretched from eastern New York to northeastern Ohio, and from southern Ontario to northern Pennsylvania. But the boundaries were loose. The Iroquois sometimes traveled as far west as the Mississippi River, as far south as Tennessee, and as far north as Hudson Bay.

When we learn about their society, it seems very different from ours. But like all people, they fed, clothed, and housed themselves; educated their children; set up a working government; played favorite sports and games; and had national celebrations. Like most peoples, they fought wars when necessary, and hoped for peace.

Many history books are about the Iroquois and the settlers — trade, the sharing of skills and knowledge, the spread of contagious diseases that killed thousands of people, wars, treaties, victories, and defeats.

This book is mostly about Iroquois life before all that. It's about what it was like to grow up in one of the most powerful Indian nations in America's history before the colonists arrived.

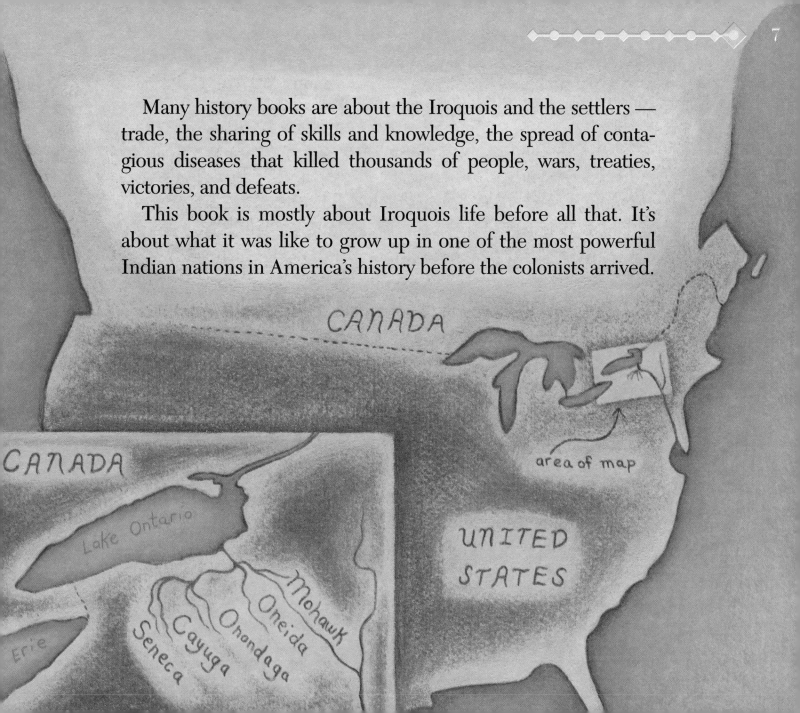

CANADA

area of map

CANADA

Lake Ontario

UNITED
STATES

Erie

Seneca

Cayuga

Onondaga

Oneida

Mohawk

Which nations made up the Iroquois League?

In the beginning, five nations made up the League: the Mohawk, Oneida, Onondaga, Cayuga, and Seneca. During colonial times, only the French called them the Iroquois. The British called them the Five Nations. And they called themselves the Haudenosaunee, the People of the Long-house.

Each nation also had a special name that related to where it lived. The Mohawk were the People of the Flint Country, because of all the flint rock in the earth. Within the League they were also known as the Keepers of the Eastern Gate, since they were the easternmost nation. The Oneida were the People of the Standing Stone, a great rock in Oneida country.

The Onondaga were the People on the Hills. Within the League they were called the Keepers of the Council Fire because they presided over the League council meetings. The

Cayuga were the People at the Boat Landing, or the People at the Mucky Land. Historians think this refers to marshland at Lake Cayuga. The Seneca were the People of the Great Hill, and also the Keepers of the Western Gate.

In the early 1700s, the Tuscarora nation, driven by settlers from its lands in the Carolinas, asked to join the League. They were accepted, and the British then called the League the Six Nations.

Through peace treaties and war, many tribes came under the protection of the Iroquois. At one time there were more than sixty other tribes that had joined the Great League.

What was the Iroquois Trail?

The trail was a path that ran through the forests and over hills, streams, and rivers, between what are now the cities of Albany and Buffalo in New York State. It was sometimes thought of as the center aisle down the Great Longhouse of the Iroquois League.

The path was wide enough for one person. It was a foot deep in some places, beaten down from so many footsteps. The trail connected the Five Nations.

The Iroquois were famous runners, and a good message runner could travel fifty or more miles in a day. But the trail was not only used to send messages. People loved to travel, and they often visited relatives in other places. The trail was also part of a great marketplace — people living far from each other could travel and trade goods and supplies.

The great trail was so well placed, the New York State Thruway today follows its path.

Did the Iroquois have a written language?

No. They had what is called an oral tradition. Their "great books" weren't read. They were told by storytellers.

Without a written language, you learn the history of your family, your village, your nation, the Great League, and the world through storytelling. Because older people were highly respected, they were usually the storytellers. There were also storytellers who traveled throughout the land. They were always invited to stay in a village for a while.

From their earliest days, children learned the old stories. Some grew up to be storytellers themselves. To be a great storyteller, you had to train your memory. Some legends, laws, and treaties could take days to recite.

There were also hundreds of fables that could be told. They were fabulous tales — about a race of little people who lived in the earth and were so powerful they could tear out the roots of an oak tree and use the tree for an arrow; about monster mosquitoes, stone giants, witches, and floating heads that streamed through the forests.

In the old tradition, the elders had a saying that you only told stories during the winter, not the summer, because people would stop work to listen. They said that birds, hearing the fables, would forget to fly, and all other animals would stop storing food for winter. In fact, the whole world

would come to a halt because everyone loves to listen to a good tale. And if that happened, there'd be no corn, no beans, no squash, or other food to store for the long, cold months.

And that's why, as the story goes, you should only tell stories in the winter.

Did everyone speak the same language?

The Five Nations spoke different dialects of the Iroquois language. Often they understood one another; sometimes they didn't. But they were able to quickly learn each other's dialects, since they shared a common language.

Throughout New York State and parts of the Midwest, we use Iroquois names for different geographic places — Schenectady, Genesee, Oswego, Canajoharie, and Ohio, for example. Other Northeast Indian words, some Iroquois, some Algonquin — such as porcupine, wampum, and raccoon — have also become part of the English language.

What was wampum?

Beads cut from seashells were called wampum. Indians living in eastern Long Island were the original wampum makers. They supplied the beads to the Iroquois. Most often the Iroquois used purple, white, and black beads.

Some people think wampum was used like money. In the old days before the Europeans came, wampum was *never* used for money. The Iroquois used the beads to make strings and belts that had special purposes. The beads were woven into different picture patterns.

Wampum strings were used in the Condolence Ceremony, the religious ritual performed when someone dies. Messengers always carried wampum strings or belts. When they showed the wampum, the listener knew the messengers' words could be trusted. It was as if by carrying wampum, a messenger had taken an oath that he was speaking the truth.

What other ways was wampum used?

The Iroquois also used wampum belts to record important information and great events: the founding of the League, the laws governing the League, treaties with other nations, and other stories. The great collection of wampum belts was kept by the Onondaga nation, who were called the Wampum keepers.

The story of the creation of the League and some treaties are as long as a two-hundred- or a three-hundred-page book. They take days to recite. It is said that the designs on certain wampum belts represent these stories and treaties. On special occasions, the belts are "read" aloud. The designs help the person reciting to remember all the words.

Where would you live?

You lived in a village, often built on high ground and surrounded by an oval-shaped stockade. The stockade was made of logs about twenty feet tall. You entered through an opening where the logs overlapped. Farm fields surrounded the village.

Inside the stockade there were rows of buildings. Most of the buildings were longhouses, and that was your home.

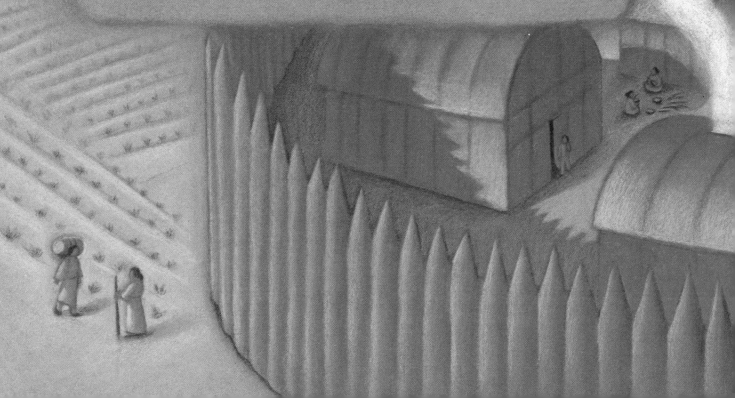

What was a longhouse?

A longhouse was just that — a long house. It was made of upright logs and cross poles, and covered with elm bark. The longhouse had a curved roof of saplings bent over from one side of the longhouse to the other. There were no windows, but there were fire holes along the center of the roof that let out smoke from cooking fires.

The longhouses were fifteen to twenty feet high and about twenty feet wide. They were usually between fifty and one hundred and fifty feet long, depending on how many families lived in one. (One hundred and fifty feet is half the length of a football field.) It was easy for a new family to move in — you just added an extension to the end.

What did the inside of a longhouse look like?

When you lifted the bark door attached at the top, you looked down a center aisle all the way to the other end. This aisle was about eight feet wide. Just inside the door there were food storage barrels and stacks of firewood. At the far end of the longhouse was another storage area.

On either side of the center aisle were compartments about thirteen feet long and six feet wide. You and your family would live in one of these. The compartments were separated from each other by skin or bark partitions sometimes made into closets.

Wooden platforms for storage and sleeping lined the walls of each compartment. Some closets had sleeping bunks for little children. You sat and slept on corn husk mats, and covered yourself with deer or bear skins.

Each family had its own cooking utensils, bowls, spoons, bows and arrows, clothing, blankets, and other items. Most things were stored in baskets and bags under the bunks.

Fires were lit in shallow pits in the center aisle. Your family cooked there and shared the fire with the family on the other side of the aisle.

Where would you bathe?

Outside the stockade was a small round-shaped sweat house where you took a steam bath, sometimes once a day.

Inside, stones were heated in a fire. Then water was poured over them, creating great billows of steam. You sat inside for as long as you could stand it, rubbed yourself with sand, and ran outside and jumped into a stream or lake.

The Iroquois, like most American Indians, cleaned themselves much more frequently than the colonists, who bathed, at most, once a week.

Would you live in the same village your whole life?
Probably not. The whole village usually moved every ten or twenty years. Sometimes there were no longer enough animals to be hunted or wild fruits to be gathered. Sometimes the farmlands were no longer good for growing crops. Sometimes so much forest land had been cleared, there wasn't enough firewood. It made sense then to move.

The villagers would find a new location and prepare the land. The men made cuts in the tree trunks all around at their base. After the tree sap stopped running, they would pack clay or mud above the cuts and then light a fire at the tree base. The clay and mud kept the fire from spreading up the trunk. Then they would chop at the burned wood until the tree fell. The men cleared land this way for both the village and the farmland.

Soon a village of new longhouses stood in the clearing, and you had a new home.

Who was in your family?

The answer may surprise you. You belonged to a "fireside family" — your parents, brothers, and sisters. But you also belonged to a longhouse family and a clan family.

You would call your mother *and* your mother's sisters all "mother." In the same way, these aunts, as we call them today, would think of you as their child.

You had lots of brothers and sisters — the ones from your fireside family *and* your mother's sisters' children *and* your father's brothers' children all were your brothers and sisters. Today we call these people cousins.

As you can see, nobody came from a small family.

What was your longhouse family?

Even more important than your fireside family was your longhouse family. A woman, usually the oldest, was the head of the longhouse family. Everyone in the longhouse family was related to her.

No matter where you lived when you grew up, you always belonged to your mother's longhouse family. Girls as adults usually stayed in the longhouse of their birth. Boys as adults moved into the longhouses of their wives, but they still belonged to their mother's longhouse family.

And so not everybody in your longhouse family lived in your longhouse. And not everybody who lived in your longhouse belonged to your longhouse family.

If this seems confusing, the most important thing to know is that the Iroquois had many more relatives they lived with, worked with, played with, learned with, and depended on than most of us do today.

What were the clans?

Two or more longhouse families made up a clan. It was believed that everybody in the clan was descended from the same female ancestor who had died a long time before. You belonged to the clan of your mother.

The clans were named after animals. Of the nine clans we know of, the most common were Wolf, Turtle, and Bear. Not every nation had every clan, but all had those three. Whenever the Five Nations met at meetings, funerals, and festivals, the clans performed important work.

The head of the clan was the oldest and most respected woman. She gave out names to everyone, decided who were to be the League council chiefs, removed them if necessary, and set the dates for the festivals.

Members of your clan were considered your relatives no matter where they lived. So, if you were in the Turtle Clan in the Mohawk Nation, you could stay with Turtle Clan people, who were considered your relatives, if you traveled hundreds of miles away to the Seneca Nation.

When did babies get their names?

That depended on when you were born. Naming ceremonies were held twice a year at two celebrations — the
Green Corn and Midwinter Festivals.

The Green Corn Festival was usually in August, and
lasted for several days. On the first day, all children born
after the Midwinter Festival were given their names.

The Midwinter Festival was usually held in early February. All children born after the Green Corn Festival were
named at this time.

Naming was a very special event. The different clans in
each nation "owned" collections of names that had been
handed down through the generations. The clan mother
kept track of all the clan's names. One Onondaga woman
has said a clan mother has "a bag of names by her side."
When someone died or changed names, the old name
went back into the clan mother's "bag."

You would probably have several names during your life. You would have one when you were born, sometimes another when you were a teenager, and another on a special occasion such as becoming a chief. If you became a League council chief, you took the name of the chief you replaced, but you did keep your own name as well.

Like other Native Americans, the Iroquois didn't have last names. In fact, people didn't usually call you by your given name. They used your nickname, and everybody had one. With relatives, you often used a family word like uncle, or younger brother, or grandmother.

What kinds of food would you eat?

You'd eat lots of vegetables, fruits, and nuts, and many different kinds of meat and fish.

Women farmed the fields surrounding the village. Although each family had its own small piece of land, the women shared the work. Certain fields were set aside to raise crops for council meetings and festivals. Everyone helped with these as well.

Corn, beans, and squash were the main vegetables. They were called the "Three Sisters, Our Supporters," and were planted together in small hills. Since corn was the main crop, some women had over one hundred and fifty corn recipes.

Bunches of braided corn were hung up to dry from longhouse rafters. Other corn was shelled and cooked. Women pounded kernels into flour. Hunters and travelers carried pouches of powdered corn mixed with maple syrup.

Where did you get meat and fish?

Hunters brought home deer, bear, beaver, rabbit, squirrel, wild turkey, and passenger pigeon. Some meat was dried and stored in clay pots or in pits lined with animal skins.

The Iroquois didn't kill for sport. They needed to hunt in order to live. Nearly everything from the hunt was used. The meat was eaten, skins made into clothing and bedding, bones used for tools and utensils, sinews for string. At certain times of the year, female animals were not hunted at all, for it was the season when they bore their young.

Iroquois men and boys were skilled fishermen, too. They often fished at night. The light from their torches would attract fish to the surface where the men could catch them easily.

How many ways would you use corn?

So many different things were done with corn, it's hard to count them all. For example:

- Dried kernels were used as beads and for decoration.
- Corn husks were used to make

  mats to sit and sleep on,

  moccasins,

  kindling,

  baskets,

  medicine masks,

  and dolls.

- Cornstalks were used as tubes to hold medicines.
- Green corn leaves were sometimes used as bandages.
- Corn silk was used to make medicines.
- Corncobs were thrown on a fire for smoking skins (see page 34).

And that's not even counting all the ways corn was cooked.

Would you eat meals with your family?

You would eat a morning meal, like breakfast, together. After that, you were on your own. Your mother would have a pot cooking all day long. Whenever you were hungry, you could get something to eat.

The Iroquois were known for their hospitality to neighbors and strangers alike. Whenever people came to the longhouse, they were offered something to eat. It was rude not to offer food to a visitor. And it was rude to refuse, even if you were full. So if you visited five families in one morning, you ate at least a little at each place.

You never saw a person starving or begging for food in an Iroquois village. So long as some people had food, no one was ever allowed to go hungry.

Did each family own the land it farmed?

No. The Iroquois, like most Native Americans, did not believe you could own, buy, or sell land. The earth was a gift from the Creator to be passed on to your children. Sometimes the Iroquois spoke of caring for the earth "to the seventh generation," which means as far into the future as you can imagine — which really means forever. Women, who worked the land, temporarily controlled it but never permanently owned it.

The Iroquois didn't measure peoples' worth by how much property or land they had. In fact, chiefs were usually among the poorest in a village. They were judged by how wise and generous they were. When chiefs received gifts, they were expected to give them away.

This was very different from the way the colonists thought about land and property. In Europe, the wealthier you were, the more powerful you were. And so when the colonists met the people of the Five Nations, there were often misunderstandings and conflicts about land and property.

What kind of clothing would you wear?

Everybody's clothing was handmade. You'd wear deerskins that the women had tanned, cut, and sewed. Like other Native Americans, the Iroquois used what nature provided and fashioned it for their needs.

Women wore long skirts that reached almost to their ankles. The skirts were decorated with beads or porcupine quills dyed red, blue, and yellow. Sometimes women wore leggings under their skirts. On top they wore a deerskin vest or blouse.

Men wore kilt-like skirts almost to their knees over leggings. They, too, wore blouses or vests made of decorated deerskins.

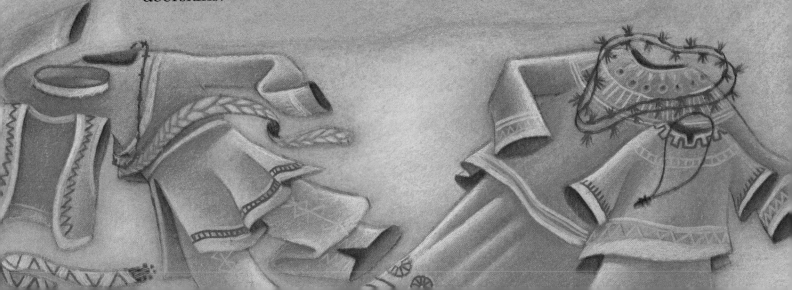

How would you prepare skins for clothing?

Before skins could be made into clothing, they needed to be tanned.

Tanning was a most interesting process. You'd use not only the skin of the deer but also its brains. The women mixed the brains with moss and formed cakes that they dried. These cakes could last for years.

To tan a skin, a woman first scraped off the hair. Then she boiled the brain cake in water, removed the moss, and soaked the skin in the solution for a few hours. She wrung the skin out and stretched it until it was dry and soft. If the skin was thick, she would repeat the process until it was ready for the next step.

At this point, the pores of the deerskin were still open, and the skin could tear easily. So the woman smoked each side of the skin over a corncob fire until the pores closed. Then the skins were ready to be cut and stitched into clothing.

What kinds of shoes would you wear?

Everyone wore moccasins, which were strong, comfortable, and often decorated with special designs. They were made of one piece of deerskin that had a seam at the heel and in front above your foot. There was never a seam on the bottom, for it would have been uncomfortable. The moccasin was sewn together with a deer-bone needle, using sinew from the deer for thread.

What shoes were good in winter?

In the winter, you would use a special kind of shoe with your fur-lined moccasins — a snowshoe. Snowshoes were an Indian invention. They were nearly three feet long and about sixteen inches wide. They were made from pieces of hickory wood bent round at the top. The netting was made of deer leather.

Snowshoes were particularly useful on hunting trips. A moose or deer would move slowly as it sank through the snow crust, while the hunter in his snowshoes walked quickly on the surface.

How would you wear your hair?

Women and girls wore their hair in two braids until they were married. Then they would usually wear one braid and tie it up with a ribbon or ornament.

Men and boys, ages fifteen and up, often had only a strip of hair on the top of their heads. Today we call this a Mohawk haircut, but, in fact, men in many tribes in the eastern United States wore their hair this way.

They didn't shave their heads; they pulled the hairs out. Men and boys also plucked their facial hair. As the hair on the chin and above the upper lip began to grow, they would pull it out, sometimes with their fingers, sometimes using clam shells as tweezers. Beards and mustaches made you look too much like a furry animal, people said.

How were you punished if you did something wrong?

If you did something bad, you were never spanked. Water might be thrown on you, or you might be dunked in a stream. If you were really bad, you knew "Longnose" would come after you. He threatened to carry you off unless you promised to be good.

Longnose was an adult, usually a relative, who wore a special mask that every child knew and feared. When Longnose came after you, you always promised to change your behavior.

How were grown-ups punished for committing crimes?

Not many people committed crimes, and so there were no jails or police. Hardly anyone ever stole anything. There were no locks on longhouse doors. A stick or a pole leaning across a door was a sign that no one was home and others should stay out. Inside the longhouse, all possessions were stored in open areas. Stealing, however, was so shameful, everyone looked down on a thief. And that was considered a very strong punishment.

A few crimes would be severely punished. Murder, the worst crime of all, was punishable by death. When a murder occurred, the nations or clans involved held meetings to try to prevent revenge attacks. The murderer's family might send a present of white wampum to the victim's family. This was a sign of a confession and an asking for forgiveness. If the wampum was accepted, the murderer was forgiven. If it wasn't accepted, the victim's family had a right to punish the murderer.

Would you go to a doctor when you got sick?

There were different kinds of healers who could treat you. It all depended on your illness. The Iroquois believed you could become ill from bad food or water or air, or by catching someone else's disease. But they also believed you could become sick because of witchcraft by bad people, or by the work of evil spirits.

Sometimes when you were sick, the False Faces or one of the other medicine societies would try to heal you. These medicine groups performed special rituals that are still an important part of the religion. (The Iroquois believe other people should not know about these ceremonies.)

You never paid the healers. Instead, you offered them sacred tobacco and gave them the kinds of food they liked. The False Faces favored a certain kind of pudding. Another medicine group, the Little Water Society, loved boiled bear's head and corn syrup. If you were cured, you became a member of the society and helped to treat others.

If you broke your leg or arm, you'd be treated by a surgeon. The Jesuit priests who traveled among the Iroquois in the 1600s wrote in their diaries that the Iroquois were excellent surgeons who not only set broken bones, but also understood the importance of keeping wounds clean. Not many European doctors practiced strict cleanliness in those days.

If you had a cold, fever, chills, snakebite, or some similar sickness, an herbalist would probably treat you. The herbalist was usually an older woman who knew which plants could be used for healing.

Certain roots, for example, cured rattlesnake bites. And very strong tea made of maple bark would help if you had a stomachache. You could also soak maple leaves in hot water and use them like a heating pad to get rid of a boil. The knowledge about plants was handed down from grandmothers to mothers to their daughters, and on and on.

Many of our medicines today are made from plants. That's one reason some people are working so hard to save the rain forests, for many medicinal plants grow there. Researchers in laboratories make other medicines, often copying the way plants work.

There are scientists and others who are trying to find Native Americans who still have the ancient medicine plant knowledge. They believe there is much we can learn from the old ways that can help us today.

How would you know the time or date if you didn't have a clock or a calendar?

The Iroquois didn't measure time the way we do today. They marked the passage of time by the rising and setting of the sun and the changes in the moon. It takes about a month for a new moon to reach its first quarter, become full, and finish its last quarter.

The Iroquois had different names for the moon at different times of the year, depending on what was happening in nature. We don't know the very old names, but these are some Mowawk names we do know: The April–May moon is *Oneratoka* — or promise of nature. The September–October moon is *Saskekowa* — last warning for the harvest. And the December–January moon is *Tsotorha* — starting to freeze.

People didn't need calendars, for example, to know when the Midwinter Festival would begin. When they were away from home, hunters watched for a group of seven stars that we call the Pleiades. They are winter stars that only appear in the eastern sky after the first frost. The Pleiades set in the west around the time of the last frost. When they are directly overhead, the time of frost is half over. That was the sign that the Midwinter Festival would occur five days after the next new moon.

And so the Iroquois didn't need clocks or calendars. They carefully watched the sun, moon, stars, and earth. And they lived their daily lives in unison with the world as it changed around them.

Would you go to school?

You wouldn't go to a school building. In fact, you wouldn't go to any formal school. You learned by watching grown-ups hunt and farm, tan hides and carve bowls, make bows and arrows and beaded moccasins, and create and build all other things.

You learned about Iroquois history and the founding of the Great League when elders told the story of the Peacemaker and Hiawatha at the festivals. (This was not the same Hiawatha in the Longfellow poem *The Song of Hiawatha.*) During the long winter months, children sat around the fire and listened as their elders told fabulous tales. There were tales about good people and very foolish ones. Some of the stories were funny, some were sad, and some were very scary. All had a meaning you could think about.

Who were your teachers?

Until boys were eight or nine years old, they stayed with their sisters, mothers, and aunts. When they grew older, they spent some time with their fathers. But often their most important teachers were their mother's brothers (their uncles). From these older men, boys learned the ways of the forest — how to hunt, make tools, and build longhouses and canoes. Girls learned many things from their mothers and aunts — how to make clothing, cultivate the soil, plant seeds, and bring in the harvest.

You also learned from your own experiences. As teenagers, both boys and girls went into the forest alone. You stayed in a small hut and you didn't eat any food for days. If you had a vision or special dream, what you dreamed about became your guardian spirit, a spirit you believed would protect and watch over your life.

What kind of work did people do?

Nobody ever asked the question, "What do you want to do when you grow up?" You knew what you were going to do. Work was part of everyday life.

Unlike today when a person's job may be just one part of a whole process, with the Iroquois, you usually did everything. For example, if you work today in a basket-making factory, you might do only one thing, such as prepare the base. But an Iroquois girl or woman did the *whole* job: She made the tools she needed for the work; she gathered and prepared the materials; and then she actually made the whole basket.

There was no such thing as a job people looked down on. Every job was respected.

Work also depended on the season:

- In the spring, you would peel elm bark for longhouses and canoes, tap trees for maple syrup, pick strawberries when they ripened, and catch fish.

- When the ground was ready for planting, you'd sow seeds for all the vegetables.
- In the late summer and fall, you'd harvest the crops and prepare them for storage.

- In the fall, you'd begin hunting and continue through part of the winter.

- During the winter, you'd spend a good deal of time indoors, making and repairing clothing, tools, bowls, baskets, and instruments of all kinds.

Girls and women, and boys and men often did different kinds of work. Men made tools for hunting and weapons for war. They made wampum and carved wooden bowls, cups, and stone pipes. They also made sports equipment and musical instruments.

Women made clay pots and baskets, cradleboards for carrying babies, clothing and moccasins, which sometimes had elaborate decorations, and many other things.

Although women and men often worked on different things, there was also a great deal of cooperation. For instance, men cleared the farmland while women were the actual farmers. When men hunted, they used woven straps women had made to carry home their game. And when women made baskets, men crafted the handles.

Work was something everybody did. You didn't work for money and you didn't work for someone else. You worked and made things for yourself and your community. In fact, you made just about everything in life you needed and used.

What games would you play?

Everybody loved sports and games. There were many team games. One of the most popular was lacrosse, which was called "the ball game." At festivals and other celebrations, sometimes one village or one clan challenged another. Even nations played against one another. Players often trained and ate special diets to prepare for big games.

There were usually six to eight players on a team. They lined up in two rows facing each other. Each player had a bat. The ball was dropped between the two lines, and each team fought for possession. You'd run with the ball in the bat's netting until you were blocked. Then you'd hurl the ball to another team player. If you carried the ball through your own team's gate a set number of times, your team would win. As with all Iroquois team games, individual players weren't thought of as stars. It was the team's victory that was important.

During everyday life, runners carried information from one village or nation to another. So it's not surprising that running was also a sport. Trained runners often competed at festivals. Sometimes a race would be the entertainment ending one of the Grand Council meetings.

Would you play games of chance?

The Iroquois loved these kinds of games. They would often bet on the outcome of any contest. One favorite was a game played with beans made of polished elk horn. They were about an inch in diameter and burned on one side to make them dark-colored. You'd put eight in a bowl and toss them. If six turned up the same color, you got two points. Less than six, no points; seven, four points; all the same color, twenty points. There was a pile of extra beans on the side. The winner received a bean for every point.

A similar game was played with six peach stones blackened on one side and shaken in a bowl. The peach-stone game was often played on the last day of the Green Corn, Harvest, and New Year's Festivals.

Were there special wintertime games?

In winter, snow-snake was probably the most popular game. You played with a five- to nine-foot-long polished hickory stick that was the "snake." The head was about an inch wide, rounded, and turned up slightly. The back end tapered down to about half an inch.

You prepared a track by dragging a log for about a third of a mile through the snow. Then you'd sprinkle water on the track to make it icy. You held the snake in your right hand and supported it with your left. You'd run a few steps and hurl it down the track. The hard part was to throw it in an absolutely straight line so that it wouldn't get stuck in a snowbank. Whichever team threw the snake the farthest for a set number of times won.

What were the traditional religious beliefs?

The Iroquois believed the Creator, or Great Spirit, made the world. They have a creation story much like the Judeo-Christian Garden of Eden story.

They also believed that almost all natural things were under the care of spirits. There were spirits of the wind, clouds, rain, trees, plants, medicines, and more. These spirits were not worshiped as gods. They were assistants to the Great Spirit. With the spirit world all around, religion was a part of everything in life.

The Iroquois had no special religious leaders like priests, ministers, or rabbis. But each nation had Keepers of the Faith in charge of religious festivals. When you had that duty, your name was changed and you received a new one. Keepers of the Faith were ordinary men and women with no special privileges, costumes, or rewards. But they did have special responsibilities. They organized the festivals and performed some of the rituals.

Religious ceremonies could last for hours. Some festivals lasted for days. There was always an offering of thanks to the Creator and all of nature.

This is one part of the Thanksgiving Address called "Greetings to the Natural World" that has been published in a booklet:

We are all thankful to our Mother, the Earth, for she gives us all that we need for life. She supports our feet as we walk about upon her. It gives us joy that she continues to care for us as she has from the beginning of time. To our Mother, we send greetings and thanks. *Now our minds are one.*

Did everyone practice the same religion?

Most people shared the same religious beliefs. But let's say you had been captured and adopted by an Iroquois family. If in your original home you had practiced a different religion, you could continue to do so. The Iroquois respected others' religions. They did not try to force their beliefs on anyone. In fact, their constitution, the Great Law of Peace, guaranteed freedom of religion.

How did the Iroquois believe the world began?

In the Iroquois story, like the biblical story of creation, Earth was made before there were people. The creation story has been told for centuries. Today there are at least forty versions. Although there are small differences, they all tell the same basic story:

Before people lived on Earth, before there even was an Earth, there was a Sky-world. Below the Sky-world was a vast space of air, and below that, a great body of water. Sky-people lived in the upper world. In the center of the Sky-world stood a magnificent tree whose flowers gave out brilliant light. One day the chief of the Sky-people became ill. To help him get well, the great tree was pulled up. The chief's wife bent over to look through the hole and fell into the vast space.

When the seabirds below saw her falling, they caught her on their wings and gently lowered her down. The turtle offered to hold her, but first, earth was needed to cover his back.

The otter, beaver, and muskrat each in turn swam to the bottom of the great waters to gather soil. Only the muskrat succeeded. He placed a fistful of dirt on the back of the turtle, and it grew into the island of Earth. The birds then lowered Sky-woman onto the turtle's back.

In time, Sky-woman gave birth to a daughter, who gave

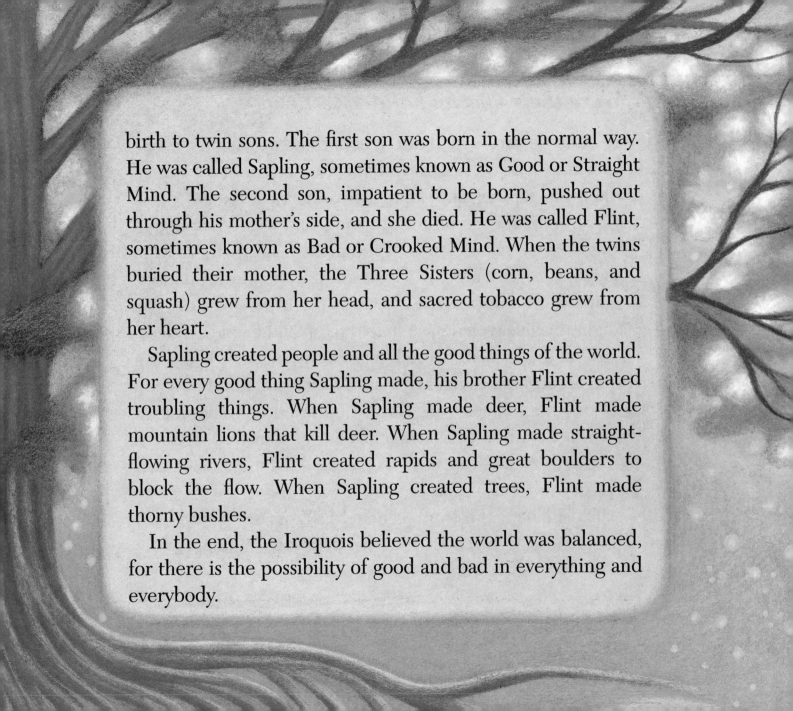

birth to twin sons. The first son was born in the normal way. He was called Sapling, sometimes known as Good or Straight Mind. The second son, impatient to be born, pushed out through his mother's side, and she died. He was called Flint, sometimes known as Bad or Crooked Mind. When the twins buried their mother, the Three Sisters (corn, beans, and squash) grew from her head, and sacred tobacco grew from her heart.

Sapling created people and all the good things of the world. For every good thing Sapling made, his brother Flint created troubling things. When Sapling made deer, Flint made mountain lions that kill deer. When Sapling made straight-flowing rivers, Flint created rapids and great boulders to block the flow. When Sapling created trees, Flint made thorny bushes.

In the end, the Iroquois believed the world was balanced, for there is the possibility of good and bad in everything and everybody.

Were there special holiday festivals?

Yes, and they were held throughout the year. The first of the six main holidays was the Maple Festival in early spring, when the sap began to flow. Everyone gave thanks to the Great Spirit for the return of spring, and to the maple tree for giving its "sweet waters." Like all the festivals, there were day-long ceremonies of speeches, prayer, music, dances, games, and always a feast. At this particular feast, as you might imagine, you'd have maple syrup and maple candies.

At all the festivals, sacred tobacco was burned. The rising smoke carried messages of thanks to the Creator. For some ceremonies, tobacco was thrown on the fire. Sometimes it was smoked. But it was not smoked every day the way some people do today. Tobacco was a sacred plant and was used only for religious purposes.

The Planting Festival occurred later in the spring. You gave thanks to the Great Spirit for the return of the planting season. And you'd ask for blessings on the seeds placed in the earth.

In late May or early June, tiny wild strawberries ripened. With them came the Strawberry Festival, which celebrated the return of the first fruits of the earth. After the long winter, it was a sweet beginning to a new year. You'd feast on fresh strawberries.

The next festival was a very big one that lasted four days. It was the Green Corn Festival, and it was usually held in August, when corn, squash, and beans were ready to eat. Everyone gave thanks to the spirits governing the Three Sisters.

During the Green Corn Festival, all children born since the Midwinter Festival would be given their names. On each day there were speeches, the Thanksgiving Address, prayers, dances, songs, and other rituals. You feasted on corn soup and succotash, which is made of corn, beans, and squash. On the last day of the festival, everyone played the peach-stone game.

The Harvest Festival was usually celebrated in early October. All the crops were picked, cooked, and stored for winter eating. Like the Green Corn Festival, it lasted for four days of prayers, songs, dances, games, and feasts.

The Midwinter or New Year's Festival, usually in early February, was the longest. It lasted seven days. The festival began when two elders visited every house in the village to announce the new year. They dressed in bear skins or buffalo robes, and had wreaths of corn husks on their heads and around their ankles and arms. In each longhouse they stirred the ashes of the old fire and told the people to clean house and light a new fire.

The Thanksgiving Address lasted for hours. Then came the dream-telling ceremony. For the Iroquois, dreams had great meaning. You described your dream in a disguised way, sometimes in riddles, and then others had to guess its meaning. For example, someone might say, "It has holes, yet it catches." This could mean a lacrosse stick, which has a net. You would only be at peace when the meaning of your dream was guessed. It was as if by understanding your dreams, you were cleaning your mind and heart, just as you cleaned the longhouse for the new year.

There was much dancing, singing, and feasting. And all the babies born since the Green Corn Festival were named.

When was the League of the Iroquois founded?

The story of the beginning of the League has been told over hundreds of years — so far back in the past that no one is certain of the date. Some believe the League was founded in the 1400s, others say earlier, still others think later. In the 1600s, Jesuit missionaries who traveled among the Iroquois believed that the League was "very ancient."

How did the League begin?

Before the League existed, the Five Nations were always at war with one another. Village fought village, and nation fought nation. It was called the time of "great sorrow and terror."

During these dark times, a man came down from the North to the Iroquois lands. His name was Deganawidah, and he was adopted by the Mohawk. Today his name is never spoken, and he is known only as the Peacemaker. The Peacemaker brought "the Good News of Peace and Power," saying that only by ending war among themselves would the nations become strong. Only through union would the people be safe.

The first person who accepted his message of peace was a woman named Jigonsasee, New Face. He called her the Mother of Nations. Then the Peacemaker met Hiawatha, an Onondaga by birth. The three set out to persuade the nations to join together in peace. The Onondaga were the hardest to convince. Tadodaho, also called Atotarho, was the most powerful

Onondaga chief. He was a very cruel and dangerous man, whose hair, it was said, twisted around his head like snakes. At first, Tadodaho opposed the idea. Hiawatha, the story goes, finally persuaded him to join, and thus "combed the snakes out of Tadodaho's hair."

The people then uprooted the tallest pine tree and threw all their weapons of war into the hole. When they replanted this Great Tree of Peace, four white roots spread out to the east, north, west, and south. The chiefs of the nations sat under the tree and met in council.

In a village, the Peacemaker said, many families live together in a longhouse, each with a separate fire. Now the Five Nations live in a Great Longhouse, each keeping its own fire (the nations remained separate), but living in peace under one roof (under one system of law). And so the Iroquois call themselves the Haudenosaunee, the People of the Longhouse.

The Peacemaker said if any other people want to obey the laws of the Great Peace, "they may trace the roots to their source . . . and they shall be welcomed to take shelter beneath the Tree." In time, some sixty tribes came under Iroquois protection.

What is the Great Law of Peace?

The Great Law of Peace is the Iroquois Constitution. Like the United States Constitution, it establishes the form of the government and sets down rules about the freedoms and duties of the people and their leaders. Like the British Constitution, it is unwritten.

The Peacemaker believed that by joining the League, the Five Nations could live together in peace. It worked. Once the Iroquois formed the League, they never again fought against one another. These are some of the ideas of the Great Law:

- All Iroquois land was open to members of the Five Nations. It was safe to travel and hunt anywhere from Mohawk lands in the East to Seneca lands in the West.
- Women as well as men participated fully in government. Women had the very important task of appointing the chiefs and removing them if they didn't properly perform their jobs.

- Freedom of religion was guaranteed to all, including other nations or individuals who joined the League.
- There was no such thing as slavery. If you were taken prisoner by the Iroquois, you were either adopted or killed. If you were adopted, you had *all* the freedoms everyone else had.

Just as the United States flag is the symbol of the American Union, the longhouse and the Great Pine Tree with its white roots are the symbols of the Iroquois League. The Peacemaker took one arrow from each of the Five Nations and tied them together. You can break one arrow, he said, but the bundle of five is too strong to destroy. The Iroquois League is, in fact, one of the world's longest lasting unions. The Great League continues to exist today in the United States and Canada.

How was the government set up?

The Iroquois government was like the American government today. Each of the Five Nations, like every American state, had its own government. Each Nation sent chiefs to the League council meetings, just as every state sends representatives to the United States Congress. Like the American government, military leaders were not allowed to be regular, or civilian, leaders. And so council chiefs could not be warriors.

Anything that concerned all the nations was discussed at the League council meetings. The council met at least once a year. No one chief and no one nation ruled over the others. A League meeting was held "across the council fire." On the east side of the fire sat the Mohawk and the Seneca, the Elder Brothers. The Oneida and Cayuga, the Younger Brothers, sat across from them on the west side. At the north were the Onondaga, the Keepers of the Council Fire. They presided over the meetings.

Everyone had to agree to all decisions, that is, all votes had to be unanimous. First, the chiefs of each nation talked among themselves and came to a decision. Then each nation discussed the decision with the other nation on their side of the fire. When the Mohawk and Seneca were in agreement, they sent their decision "across the fire" to the Cayuga and Oneida. When all four agreed, the decision was told to the Onondaga. If the Onondaga agreed,

the chief conducting the meeting announced that the League could now "speak with one voice." They had come to a unanimous decision.

If the Onondaga disagreed, the two sides across the fire discussed everything again. They might change their decision, but if they didn't, this time the Onondaga had to accept it. Only when everyone agreed, did the League "speak with one voice."

Were there special rules of behavior at the council meetings?

When a person spoke, no one interrupted with questions. In fact, you never asked questions. You made all your comments when it was your turn to speak.

Speakers held wampum strings in their hands. They used the wampum to help them remember everything they wanted to say. When they were finished, they hung the strings on a pole. The next speaker then picked them up.

Whenever a new topic was raised, you waited a full day before discussing it. That way everyone had a chance to think about it. You also ended the discussion at nightfall. If you stayed up late debating, you might lose your temper, or rush into a decision because you were tired.

The meetings took time and patience, but they created a very strong union. Since the talks only ended when everybody agreed, everyone felt they had played an important part.

All the people were encouraged to come to council meetings, not just the chiefs. And so a meeting was a great social event as well as a time for government business.

Who were the members of the League council?

When the Peacemaker and Hiawatha founded the League, there were fifty-one chiefs on the council, including the Peacemaker. The original chiefs' names became the names of the office. And so if you became a council chief, you took the name of the chief you were replacing. Because the Peacemaker's name was never used again, after the first meeting there were fifty chiefs.

In addition to the regular council members, there were also Pine Tree Chiefs. They were chosen by the council to be members because they were very smart. They were allowed to speak at meetings, but they did not vote.

How did you become a council chief?

A woman was the first person to accept the Peacemaker's message, and so the Peacemaker said women were to appoint the chiefs. The names of the council chiefs belonged to certain clans. The head woman of the clan consulted with other clan women and made the selection.

Chiefs were appointed to the council for life. But if they became ill, or didn't perform their job properly, the clan mother could remove them from office. She'd warn the chief several times. If he didn't change his behavior after the third warning, he was removed from office. When a chief died, a Condolence Ceremony was held to mourn his death and pass on the chief title to a new person.

The Iroquois government was very different from European governments. Chiefs were not like kings. It was their job to serve the people, not to rule them. Chiefs were respected because of their wisdom, not because they were all-powerful. Often the colonists didn't understand this, and believed that chiefs had more power than they really did.

What was the Condolence Ceremony?

This was a special ritual performed when someone died. A village held the ceremony after the death of one of its people. The Peacemaker, the story is told, used wampum to comfort Hiawatha, whose family had all died. The beads, said the Peacemaker, become words that carry away the sadness.

In a village, clans were divided into two groups for the ceremony. One group helped the family whose relative had died to grieve. The other offered comfort. It was said the comforters wiped away tears, and cleared the ears and throats of the mourners so they could begin to live normal lives again.

When a council chief died, the whole League held the Condolence Ceremony. The two groups were the Elder Brothers (the Onondaga joined the Mohawk and Seneca), and the Younger Brothers (the Oneida and Cayuga). They, too, helped with mourning and comforting, but the ceremony was much more elaborate. The dead chief's nation sent out runners to announce the ceremony. All the League chiefs and many people from their nations arrived at the scheduled time.

Like other ceremonies, there was a set order for the events. First everyone mourned the death of the old chief. Then they raised up a new chief to take his place. People sang songs, and delivered thanksgiving prayers and speeches. Trained speakers recited the Great Law of Peace. The names of all the council chiefs were repeated. Since these were the names of the original fifty chiefs, it was a way of saying that the League was strong and long-lasting. It had continued from the past into the present, and would go on into the future.

Was there a special way the Iroquois ended their stories?

Storytellers and orators had a very large collection of stories to choose from — the creation story, the story of the founding of the League, hundreds of fables, and many others. Whatever the tale, the speaker always ended by saying, "*Naho.*" It is finished.

Naho.

Note to the reader

Although the Iroquois League is no longer a great power, a growing number of historians believe it had a lasting effect on the American government. Benjamin Franklin, one of the drafters of the United States Constitution, greatly admired the Iroquois form of government and borrowed some of its ideas for America:

- A government with both national and local parts.
- A way of keeping any part of the government from having too much power. In our system, we call this "checks and balances."
- A democratic government in which the leaders, the chiefs, were responsible to the people, unlike the kings and queens of Europe at the time.
- A constitution, established hundreds of years before the American Constitution, that included rights of freedom of speech and religion.

In Iroquois society, women had many more rights than colonial women. In fact, Iroquois women shared responsibility for running their government. Only in the twentieth century have American women gained some of the rights that Iroquois women had centuries earlier.

And so you could say that the old Iroquois way of life still exists today, not only in Iroquois communities, but in some parts of the American system of government as well.